How to Eat a Dinner Roll

222 Bites of Dining Etiquette

Debra Carr

How to Eat a Dinner Roll
222 Bits and Bites of Dining Etiquette   by Debra Carr

Henry Carr Publishing
1120 Keystone Avenue
Lansing, MI 48911   U.S.A.
810-250-7331
debra@imageformen.net
www.imageformen.net
www.image-enhancement.us

All rights reserved. No part of this book may be reproduced or transmitted in any form or by any means, including electronic or mechanical, including but not limited to: photocopying, recording or by any information storage and retrieval system without written permission from the author, except for brief quotations in a review.

For information of special discounts for bulk purposes, please contact the author Debra Carr at;
Henry Carr Publishing
1120 Keystone Avenue,
Lansing, MI 48911 U.S.A.

810-730-7331 or debra@imageformen.net
We invite you to visit our website at:
www.imageformen.net   or www.image-enhancement.us

Book Design & Cover Photography: Debra Carr
Cover Artwork and Design: Suzette Mulnix Visual Impressions
Printed in the United States of America

Copyright © 2014
All rights reserved
ISBN-10:0991583744
ISBN-13:978-0-9915837-4-4

Dedication

To my parents Ronald and Wahnetta Carr, who always held their breath and smiled as they supported my ideas. They never said, "It won't work, or you can't" motivating me to always do more.

To my son Ryan Lowe for encouraging me, by continually saying, "Will you get the thing done?"

"One cannot think well, love well, or sleep well, if one has not dined well."
Virginia Woolf

Contents

Acknowledgements — vii

Introduction — ix

1
In the Door and to the Table
- Arriving — 13
- Taking a Seat — 15
- As the Host or Hostess — 17
- As a Guest — 19

2
At the Table
- Your Own BMW — 23
- Plates, Bowls, Mugs, Cups and Saucers — 26
- Knives, Forks, and Spoons — 28
- Silverware placement during & after dining — 31
- Glasses and Stemware — 33
- 7 Napkin Rules — 36
- Ordering Food — 38
- Two Styles of Eating — 41
- Owning Real Estate and Passing Food — 44
- How to Eat a Dinner Roll — 46
- Table Talk — 49
- The Bill Cometh — 52
- Money on the Table — 54

3.
After Dinner Bits and Bites
- How to Give a Great Toast   57
- Invitations and Thank You Notes   59
- How to Eat Certain Foods   62
- Cocktail Parties   67
- Extra Bits and Bites   69
- Conclusion   76

About the Author   77

Acknowledgement

Thank you to my good friend Kathey Batey of Spirited Presentations, the NSA-MI members, plus those in my writer's groups and dining classes who said, "Write a book to support your trainings and to help those who unknowingly self-sabotage". Thank you to my sister Pam Carr and many friends including Kevin Farley & Carrie Treder who helped me in various ways.

Thank you to the un-named faces for motivating me to write this book:
To the man at the next table, who ate his American fried potatoes with his fingers, and then sat puzzled and clueless as his disgusted breakfast date walked out of the restaurant. To others who sat near at formal affairs with bewildered looks, as they watched for cues of how to eat particular foods. And finally, thank you to the former models I lunched with many years ago, who unknowingly motivated me to polish my own dining skills.

After reading "How to Eat a Dinner Roll" may you feel comfortable in all of your dining experiences. May each of the experiences be filled with laughter, fun, great food, and good people!

"Never eat more than you can lift!"
Miss Piggy

Introduction

While growing up in a small farming community in the mid-West, the basics of dining manners were engrained in me while I was young. "Sit up straight Debra, no elbows on the table, and quit talking with food in your mouth!" You may have heard the basics too. Oh, and don't forget: "Clean up your plate, there are people starving in ……." I followed the rules, but I never tried to figure out the starving people thing. I guess I knew my parents would never send my uneaten fried liver or cooked spinach overseas.

By the time I entered High School, the town had grown to the point of supporting an A & W restaurant, 2 soda shops, three bars and a small truck stop a few miles out of town. A sit down restaurant that served more than 2 courses, was 25 to 40 minutes away.

My parents did their best to teach me good manners; however not every kid listens to everything their parents say. I was one of those kids. Many years later, while attending my first image consulting conference, I met women who were former models. They were well groomed in wardrobe, voice and manners. I remember feeling gently intimidated as I sat with them during meals.

Feeling intimidated felt very odd as throughout the years I dined in restaurants of various cuisines, enjoyed evenings at fine clubs, home parties, and at family and friends BBQ's. I had also eaten in small town diners and restaurants.

From my barbering career, my communication and listening skills were top notch. I felt at ease in carrying a conversation with anyone, plus always felt completely comfortable whenever entering a room for any event.

So, what the heck was happening? It was an odd feeling indeed. I decided that polishing my skills further would only help. Remembering my uneasiness made me think… "If I felt that way with the knowledge I had, what about others? What about those who are dating, going to weddings, or any special event? What about the adults with kids who always eat on the run, and want to teach their kids?" My experience with the models was the main motivating factor to write this book.

As a certified image consultant, image coach and trainer one of my most popular classes is "How to Eat a Dinner Roll". The class is fun, informative and interactive. Having received continual excellent feedback after teaching the class, my intent in writing "How to Eat a Dinner Roll" was to write a light hearted book loaded with dining tips, while adding value to the millions wanting to polish their social dining skills. So, regardless if you're sitting at a table with white tablecloths or one with peanut shells on the floor, along with adding good people and great food, this book will help to enhance your dining experience. Most importantly, after reading this book you will know "How to Eat a Dinner Roll".

Bon Appetite!

1.

In the Door and To the Table

"If you really want to make a friend, go to someone's home and eat with them. The people who will give you their food will give you their heart."
Cesar Chavez

Arriving

Believe it or not, there are different guidelines for arriving at an event at a private residence, or at a restaurant. Knowing when and how will keep the stresses for everyone in check on both busy and not so busy days.

At a Home:
Do: Arrive on Time.
Do: Consider taking a Host or Hostess Gift (see Extra Bits)
Do Not: Arrive more than 5 minutes early. The host or hostess may have last minute things to complete.

Arriving late:
Plain and simply: Don't. It's Rude, and Inconsiderate. Period.

Life happens: Incase of an emergency or delay, call and give the time you plan to arrive. Follow through and never expect the rest of the group to wait for you.

Restaurants:
When arriving at an event or restaurant; you will find a maître d, host or hostesses standing behind the podium in the entryway. If you have a reservation or someone is waiting for you, give your name and ask to be seated.

- If there is a wait, step back, and never crowd the podium or waiting area.
- When it's your turn to be seated; regardless of how long it's been, smile. Yes, smile, and repeat your name so they can seat you.

- If joining others and you prefer to pay the bill, tell the host or hostess to inform your server.
- To avoid conflicts, some restaurants will take your credit card information and add the bill amount after the meal.
- When the first person arrives, they should wait until the second one arrives before being seated. Please note: Depending on the location and time of day, restaurants have different requirements for guests while waiting. Some will seat you immediately while others will ask you wait until the entire group has arrived.
- When a group of two or more arrive ahead of the others, they should ask to be seated.

Check your coat, umbrella and any additional packages you may be carrying.
- Men always check their coats
- Women have the option of taking their coat to the table

If the restaurant does not have a coat check, improvise by taking them to the table. Once there, lay your jacket or coat over the back of the chair next to you, and lay packages or carried items on the seat. Many restaurants have coat hooks near the tables. If there are hooks hang your coat, hat, and umbrella on them.

Men always help women with their coats, Period.

In the Door and to the Table

Taking a Seat

In Restaurants:
In social situations when taken to the table by a maitre'd it is always ladies first, and the man follows.

If the table is in a high traffic area, or next to the music speakers, restrooms, or too close to the noisy kitchen, do not hesitate to ask for another table. Just say, "Will you please seat us in a quieter area?" If they cannot accommodate you; you can grin and bear it, or have the choice to smile and say 'thanks anyway' and leave for another restaurant.

Men seating women: A man stands on the left side of the woman's chair as she takes her seat from the right. If the table is against the wall, he will need to improvise. Men should wait to sit until all the women have been seated at the table.

At a formal dinner: There will be a host, hostess or both. Often there is a guest of honor, who will be seated to direct right of the host or hostess. If the guest of honor is a couple, the female will sit on the right of the hostess, and the man to her left.

To eliminate confusion, when six or more people are seated at the same table, there may be place cards showing you where to sit. At a small intimate gathering, if there are no place cards when dinner is called, ask the host or hostess where they would like you to sit. If the function is large, sit anywhere. You will find it is an excellent time to meet new people and create new relationships.

At a casual gathering: Sit with friends, or take a seat with people you do not know. Possibly uneasy feeling at first, you will find it is a way of meeting new people while opening up fresh ideas for conversations.

Women: Purses should be placed on your lap, on the floor, or between your body and the back of the seat. A purse is never set on the table, and should not hang on the back of the chair, as it can easily be picked up or bothersome to waiters and those walking by.

If you have been shopping and the car is not near, you can leave your bags with the coat check clerk; or set them on a seat next to you, or underneath the table.

Once at the table, do nothing until everyone arrives. If everyone except one or two people arrive by the expected time, put the napkin on your lap, and begin ordering beverages.

Extra tips for taking a Seat:
- Ask whoever invited you where they would like you to sit. If nothing is said, take any seat you like.
- The host and hostess generally sit opposite of one another.
- The better seats at the table are the ones that look into the room or at beautiful scenery through a window. If you are the host or hostess honor your guests by giving them the 'better seats'.
- Regardless of gender, the guest of honor sits to the right of the host or hostess.

As the Host or Hostess

As the host or hostess, you have specific tasks to make sure your dinner event runs smoothly. It can be a formal dinner or event, a luncheon out with friends, to a cookout or sharing chili with cornbread in your home. As the host or hostess, here are your responsibilities:

To Begin:
- Set the date, and plan the menu - choose the restaurant by knowing your guests well. Be mindful if they adventurous in tastes, or possibly vegetarians.
- Make a guest list of people who compliment one another.
- Depending on the event, invite guests by either mail, email or by calling.
- Plan great food, and the beverages of your choice. If applicable have good music.
- When first arriving at a restaurant tell the Maître d you would like the check at the end of the meal.
- Greet every guest as they arrive. When at a restaurant if some guests are more than 8 to10 minutes late don't wait; seat the group, and order.
- Start conversations by introducing guests to one another.

At a dinner table:
- When applicable, make an opening toast to welcome guests and to begin eating.
- Fill in 'quiet moments' at the table by asking questions to continue conversations.

- Unless it is a fixed menu, subtly mention items at the mid to high range you have enjoyed, and what you will be ordering. Tell guests they can order what they would like.
- So guests feel comfortable when ordering, identify an appetizer or something else saying; how good it looks or tell of an item you have previously enjoyed.
- If meals arrive at different times, suggest the guests to start eating while the food is hot.
- If an error is made by the kitchen or wait-staff, tell the guest you will handle it, and speak to the server quietly and politely.
- After dinner say a prepared toast to the guest of honor, or have someone arranged to do so.
- At the end of the meal if there is no guest of honor, thank guests for coming and invite them to stay for conversation, coffee, or after dinner cocktails if served.
- When the check arrives, discretely review the check. Make no mention of the cost. Signal the waiter you are ready to pay by placing the check holder to the edge of the table with the credit card and bill sticking out.
- If paying the bill in cash, tell the waiter if you would like them to keep the change.
- In a casual setting, invite the guests to take part in games or other activities you have planned.
- See your guests to the door.

As the Guest

Whenever you are a guest at a formal, informal dinner or a casual cookout, you have your own "guest responsibilities." Your tasks are fun, enjoyable and simple. Here they are:

- When dining at a restaurant or an event, arrive on time or 5 to 10 minutes early.
- At a private home the rule changes. Arrive on time, and never early to allow the owners time for any last minute touches.
- Do not be late.
- If an emergency arises call, and tell the host or hostess when you plan to arrive.
- When you first arrive, meet the host or hostess.
- Bring a host or hostess gift.
- Be positive, mingle and take part in conversations with other guests.
- Keep your conversation light, friendly and enjoyable.
- Limit yourself to one or two drinks.
- Ask the host or hostess where they would like you to sit.
- In a restaurant without a set menu, or options suggested by the host or hostess order from the mid- to upper priced section. *As a guest, never order the most expensive meal.*
- Understand your 'table real estate'
- When eating family style, once the meal begins; ask if anyone would like any of the

items on the table in-front of you. Then take the initiative to start passing them to the right.
- Do not overstay and leave when most guests do.
- When it's time to leave, thank the host or hostess for inviting you and for the meal.
- Call, or send a note the following day to thank the host or hostess for inviting you. Keep it short and simple. (see Extra Bits and Bites)
- At a private home, never take pictures of the home without permission of the owners. If permission is granted, never post on any social media site without their knowledge.

"Life itself is a proper binge"
Julia Child

2.

At the Table

"There's a difference between dining and eating. Dining is an art. When you eat to get the most of your meal, to please the palate as well as satiate the appetite, that my friend, is dining"
Yuan Mei

At the Table

Your own BMW

At banquets and events the beautiful tables are often set very close together, and the chairs even closer. There have been many times I have sat so close to others I have had to double check so not to drink out of the wrong glass or eat someone else's dinner roll.
If this sounds familiar; all you have to do is look down at the place setting in front of you. Yes, it is very simple. Look down and think the letters **BMW**.

BMW

B Bread
M Meal
W Water and all liquids

The **B**read plate will always be on the left

The **M**eal is always in the middle

The **W**ater and liquids will always be on the right

Solids will be the left, and liquids will always on the right. With that said; next to the plate the forks for solids will always be on the left, and spoons will always be on the right. Other than balancing the looks of the place-setting and having it readily available for right handed people, I have no idea of the reason the knife is placed on the right.

If you remember the initials, **BMW** you will do excellent and automatically know which glass, silverware or plate is yours. It will also help you whenever you set any table. Depending on the formality of the occasion, the amount of utensils and dinnerware will change. Regardless, the basics will always stay the same.

On the next page, you will see the only difference between formal and informal place settings is: At formal dinners, the place-setting will have more pieces and the dessert fork or spoon could be placed above the dinner plate. Nothing more…that is all.
Simple? Yes!

BMW's are fun. Remembering the initials will help you to make the sea of place settings easier to maneuver through.

"My mother's menu consisted of two choices:
Take it, or Leave it."
Buddy Hackett

At the Table

INFORMAL

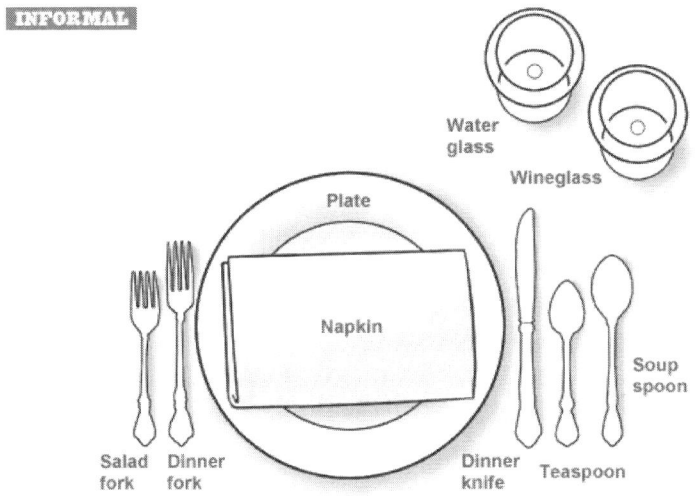

Utensils are placed one inch from the edge of the table

FORMAL

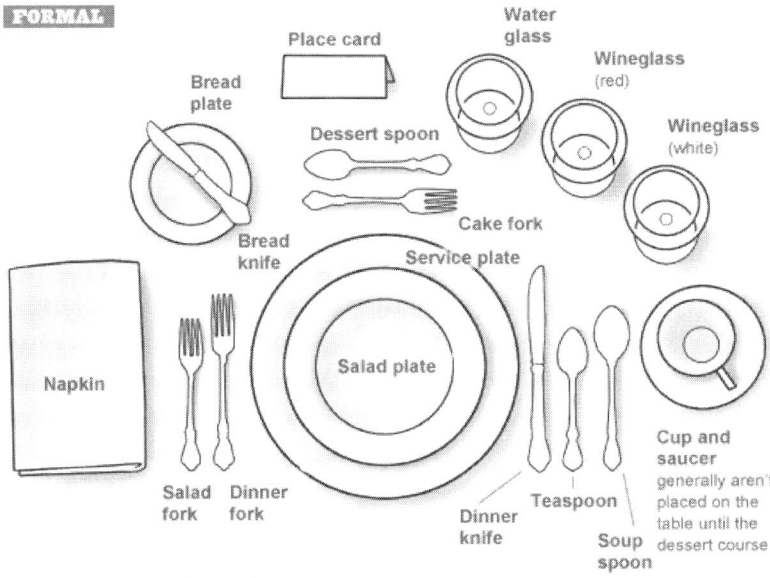

Image:source: Bewhatyoulove.com

25

Plates, Bowls, Mugs, Cups and Saucers

Regardless how often you entertain, or if you eat predominately at home or in restaurants, it is wise to know the basics of dinnerware. Dinnerware comes in all shapes, sizes and colors, plus thicknesses. From decorative paper, wood, glass or stoneware to fine china, dinnerware can add a punch of color to your table or display pure elegance. I enjoy entertaining and good food. My everyday dinnerware is Fiesta Dinnerware. It's colorful and can be mixed with other pieces to shake things up. It's great to use anytime, especially with family and friends. To add a bit of elegance, I also have a set of china that is off white with a platinum band. The style is perfect for me, as it is not so delicate to be concerned about it breaking when using it. Dinnerware can make a difference in the presentation of food, plus creates an interest while entertaining, I encourage you to only buy dinnerware in styles you love.

Chargers or Service Plates
Charger plates are oversized plates that go under soup, salad and dinner plates. Since they are used for presentation only, they are generally removed after guests are initially seated, or can be kept on the table throughout the meal. It is suggested removing chargers during dessert, since the charger plate is significantly larger than dessert plates.

Soup Bowls
Soup bowls are always brought to the table on a small serving plate. While eating soup or when finished, the small plate underneath the bowl serves as a place to rest the soup spoon.

Bread and Butter Plate
The bread and butter plate is a small plate at the top left of the dinner plate.

Salad Plate
The salad plate is to the left of the dinner plate; directly above the forks or on top of the charger/ service plate.

Dinner Plate
The dinner plate is in the center of all the silverware. During formal settings, it may sit on the charger.

Dessert Plate
Smaller in size, the dessert plate is brought to the table when dessert is served.

Mugs and Cups and Saucers
For many there is nothing better than starting the day with a good cup of coffee in their hand. Mugs can be filled with soup, chili, coffee or tea. Rugged and heavier they are used for more casual dining. Cups with saucers are used for drinking tea, or coffee and are used with fine dinnerware.

"The only time to eat diet food is while you're waiting for the steak to cook."
Julia Child

Knives, Forks and Spoons

Like other pieces in a place-setting, often the amount of eating utensils on a table can be overwhelming. You may wonder, where do I begin? If you were told to start using your utensils from the outside and work your way in toward the plate, you were told right. Once a course is completed, the silverware, plates or bowls to that course will be cleared away by the wait-staff. This is a cue to start with the next piece of silverware and continue working toward the plate. The big fork is for the entree; and the big spoon for the soup. A salad and entrée fork, teaspoon and entrée knife, are generally used during lunch in restaurants. At a formal occasion or in a fine restaurant, a salad knife, plus possibly a fish fork and the dessert silverware will be added.

The Butter Knife
This small knife rests across the top of the bread plate when not in use. Used to serve butter from the butter dish, it is also used to butter your dinner roll, bread, or croissant.

Meat or Entrée Knife
On the right, next to the dinner plate rests the largest knife; the entrée knife. This knife can double as a salad knife if one is not provided.

Salad Knife
The salad knife is a smaller knife located next to the soup spoon. Often one is not provided during lunch, but can be requested.

Fish Knife
The fish knife is easily recognizable. Smaller in size, it was designed with a curved pointed tip on the end to help ease in removing the backbone of the fish.

Teaspoon
Perfect for coffee, tea, cereals and used when tired of chasing peas on your plate, the teaspoon is narrow shaped and not very deep. If not in the original place-setting when first sitting down, it is brought to the table when coffee or dessert is served.

Soup Spoon
The soup spoon is the largest spoon and is located to the right of the knives. When soup is ordered from a menu, the spoon may be delivered when the soup is served.

Dinner or Entrée Fork
Next to the plate on the left, the Entrée fork is the largest of forks. It is used when eating a salad as an entrée, or any main course. It can be doubled as a side salad fork if one is not available.

Salad Fork
With shorter tines, the salad fork is located to the left of the plate and the furthest from the plate.

Fish Fork
Unique looking, the fish fork is a slimmer three pronged fork located between the salad and large entrée fork.

Dessert Fork or Spoon
Any utensils placed horizontally above your plate are for dessert. A spoon will show the dessert will be a pudding constituency, such as custard, soufflé, or ice cream. If both are above the plate, the spoon will be used for coffee, and the fork will show the dessert will be a cake, pie or something else such as an éclair. Often the dessert silverware will be brought at the same time as the dessert.

"You don't need a silver fork to
eat good food"
Paul Prudhomme

Silverware Placement: During and After Dining

Have you ever left the table during dinner only to return and find your meal has been removed? During the dinner and when your meal is finished using these tips will cue the wait-staff to leave your meal on the table until you are finished.

- Once a piece of silverware has been used, it should be placed on a plate or in a bowl and never go back on the table.
- While taking a break while eating, rest your fork and knife entirely on the plate.
- When finished eating, place the fork and knife diagonally on the plate, tines down, side by side, with the handles at 4 o'clock.
- The knife blade should always face the center of the plate, not point out toward another guest, which was once thought as sign of aggression. This will cue the wait staff that you are done eating and to remove your plate and silverware.
- At the end of the meal, any unused silverware not removed by the wait-staff is left in its original place.

Ice Tea Spoon
Should be placed on the saucer or to the right of the service plate/charger.

Soup Spoon
The soup spoon should be placed on the right side of the soup bowl on the service plate when finished eating.

Salad Fork and Salad Knife
Place the salad fork with the tines down and knife on the service plate underneath the salad bowl. If there is no service plate, place both pieces of silverware in the salad bowl.

Entrée Fork and Knife
When you are completed with your meal, rest your knife and fork diagonally with tines down with the handles at 4:00. When eating continental style, the finished position is the same. (For further clarification see: Two Styles of Eating)

"When in doubt, ingest carbs!"
Rachael Cohn

Glasses and Stemware

Glassware and Stemware have several functions other than holding liquid. They can be used for holding appetizers, your favorite beverage or a dessert. For now, let's forget about glasses and mugs in closets and cupboards holding change, keys, or other non–edible items.

To some people, initially walking into an eloquent dinner and seeing a mass of glassware on the table can be overwhelming. If you have ever felt confused with which glass is yours, this bite of etiquette will help you understand the sea of glassware and stemware.
Once again, remember the letters: **B M W**
Bread **M**eal **W**ater

W is on the right, which means all your liquids will always be on the right.

- The water goblet is always the largest glass, and is always above the knife.
- The wine glasses will be lined up to the right or below the water goblet according to each course.
- When drinking wines during courses start with the bottom glass and work your way up per course served. The wait-staff will remove the glass after each course.
- Your water goblet will always stay on the table for you to drink from at any time.
- If you prefer to not drink any alcohol, do not turn the glass over. Instead when the wine is about to be poured, put your hand near or above the glass and say "no thank you".

You can drink beverages from any style of glass-ware, however, matching the glass to its purpose can add elegance and enjoyment to a meal. The size of the bowl diameter has a function; allowing different types of wines to breathe. One style of glassware for wine is now stem-less. Although often sold for white wine, they should be used with red wines, as they absorb the heat of the hand when being held, raising the temperature of the wine. Placed near the upper right corner of the plate, in varying angles the glasses and stemware from the bottom glass up are as follows:

White Wine: To hold lighter wines, the bowl of the white wine glass is generally smaller and slightly straighter near the top. To keep the chilled wine cool while drinking, hold the glass by the stem.

Bordeaux: This glass is a bit shorter with a large round bowl, narrowing at the top. Hold this glass by the bowl, because red wines are served at a warmer temperature than whites so the heat of the hands will not affect the wine.

Burgundy: The Burgundy wine glass has the roundest bowl, and more open at the top than the Bordeaux. The larger bowl allows the wine to breathe. This glass is held by the bottom of the bowl.

Champagne: Often called a champagne flute; to maintain the champagne bubbles it will always be straighter and narrower than other pieces of stemware. It may have a tulip end. Since Champagne is served chilled, a champagne flute is held by the stem.

Water Goblet: Largest of all and sturdy stemmed, it is wide at the top with a deep belly. The water goblet stays on the table throughout and after the meal. Directly above the entrée knife, you will find it at the top of the glassware.

"I always knew food and wine were vital, with my mother being an Italian and a good cook"
Robert Mondavi

7 Napkin Rules

Napkin rules… Seriously? Does this compare to having the right amount of items in the 12 item line at the grocery store? Where are the image police? Does it truly make a difference where a napkin goes?

That is what I thought when taking a dining class. Yes, there are guidelines when using napkins at a table or while attending a casual BBQ. The rules are especially important when dining in a restaurant or at a social or business engagement; as it gives the waiters a cue if you are leaving the table temporarily, or are completely finished with your meal.

So, what are the 7 rules of the Napkin? When you sit down at the table to eat, the first thing you should do is put your napkin on your lap.

- Pick the napkin off the table. Then without snapping, open it.
- Fold larger napkins in ½ and place the folded edge toward your body.
- Regular size napkins are placed open on your lap.
- Use a napkin to dab only the corners of your mouth. Never blow your nose or groom with it.
- Once the napkin has been on your lap, it should never touch the table top until the end of the meal. If you leave the table temporarily, place the napkin on the seat where you've been sitting.

- At the end of the meal, the napkin should be slightly folded (never wadded) and placed on the LEFT side of your plate. If the plates have been removed, set it where the forks were originally.
- If you drop your napkin on the floor at a private residence, pick it up and ask for a clean one. If you drop one in a restaurant, leave it and ask the wait-staff for a fresh one.

The rules sound simple don't they?
One last thing; in many of the more formal restaurants the waiters may place the napkin on your lap for you. Feeling odd initially, just relax and enjoy the service.

"All sorrows are less with bread"
Miguel de Cervantes

Ordering Food

Knowing what to order can be difficult or easy. There are times you can walk into a restaurant and know immediately what you want to order. When you're exceptionally hungry everything can look good, while other times the menu may appear boring. Does this sound familiar?

As you look around, you may see an order at the next table that looks like perfect for you. If so, ask the waiter to tell you what it is, and order it if it sounds good. I have found when asked, most servers will tell you what they personally like. If you're not ready to take a chance, pick something you are familiar with and go with it.

As a known foodie, I often read menus. If I'm going to eat something, I want to know what it is. I like salads loaded with allot of extras, and like to know what makes the "special" special, and how it's prepared. Realizing this can be silently annoying to others, I am always mindful of who I'm with. If you are anything like me, make it easy on those you are with and scan the menu or read it online before going, so to order in a timely manner.

When eating alone: Order what you like, in the price range you are comfortable in paying.

As the host or hostess: and are paying the bill, order whatever you like and make menu suggestions to your guests.

If you are a guest: Take a hint from the host and hostess. They may make a suggestion of what they have enjoyed. If there are no suggestions order what you would like, but never the most expensive thing. Simply said, it is Rude.

Are appetizers being ordered? Possibly as a group you'll share appetizers, or you may want one for your main dish. You can follow the lead of others at the table. Unless you are adventurous, order foods you enjoy.

If you have been invited to a rib house for the "Worlds Best Ribs" and you are a vegetarian, or for "The Best Pizza in Town" and you do not eat gluten, go anyway. You will find other items that will work for you, and restaurants are generally great at 'adjusting' an order for customers.

If you are at a restaurant with fun "messy food" such as ribs, spaghetti, or a boiling pot of seafood with others joining in; order items like this at another time. The best time would be when you are with someone like an enduring mate or best friend who will share it with you, or put up with your messiness. Or naturally share it with your mother, who will always love you.

In the book *"Blink"* author Malcolm Gladwell wrote: "Glance quickly at the menu and order whatever catches your eye first. Spend no more than 2-3 seconds deciding or the quality of your choice will decline."

In *"Paradox of Choice"*, Barry Swartz wrote: "Take a menu and rip it up in 4 to 5 pieces, then order from one of the pieces ignoring the choices on the rest of the menu. You'll be happier!"

As you see, there are many ways to order food. Relax and order what appeals to you. From time to time, be adventurous and try new flavors and textures. The experience of eating good food is fun, especially when shared with the right people.

"Eating crappy food isn't a reward.
It's punishment!"
Drew Carey

Two Styles of Eating

With global travel now commonplace, people across the planet are experiencing first hand various styles of eating. Throughout the years I spent many hours with good friends from China and learned to use Chopsticks as if I was born with them in my hand. In cities large and small across the globe, the American and Continental Styles are the two basic ways of eating. Keep reading as you are invited to try both styles.

The American style is the preferred style of eating in the USA, and figuratively speaking Continental Style is predominately used in the European Countries. Both incorporate the use of the fork and knife. Easy and fun to learn, I enjoy eating Continental Style.

In the visuals below you will find the four phases of eating American Style and Continental Style. It's important when dining in a restaurant to use the finished position as it cues the wait staff when to remove your place setting.

American Style: With a knife in the right hand and fork with tines down in the left, cut 1 to 3 bite sizes pieces of meat or vegetables at a time. Lay the knife down across the top right side of the plate with the knife edge towards the center of the plate. Switch the fork with tines up from the left hand to the right and begin eating. In between bites, the fork and knife should be placed on the plate at 10:00 and 4:00. (see visual below) When ready for another bite pick them up and repeat.
American Style is "The Tines Up Style."

How to Eat a Dinner Roll

American Style

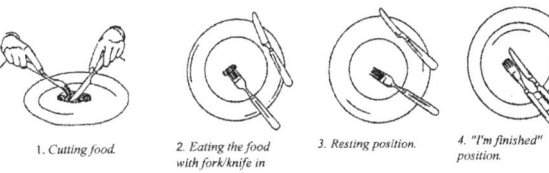

1. Cutting food.
2. Eating the food with fork/knife in right position.
3. Resting position.
4. "I'm finished" position.

Continental Style: As in American Style of eating the knife is in the right hand, and the tines down fork will be in the left. The difference between the two is: When using Continental Style, the utensils always stay in the hands during dining with the fork tines facing down. In between bites both utensils stay in the hands unless you take a drink. When taking a drink, lay both utensils down crossing the fork over the knife in the resting position. (Angle at 4:00) Mashed potatoes, vegetables and fruits are lined up along the back of the tines when eaten. Continental Style is 'The Tines Down Style.'

Continental Style

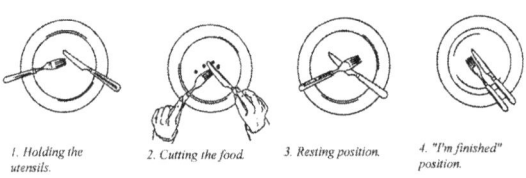

1. Holding the utensils.
2. Cutting the food.
3. Resting position.
4. "I'm finished" position.

Image source: Image Resource Group Int.

In both the American and Continental Styles, once the utensils have been used (including the handles) they never touch the table again. When finished eating, always rest forks, knives, and spoons on the plate at a 4:20 position.

At formal dinners, after each course your tableware will be taken and replaced as needed. To signal you are done with a particular course, rest your fork tines up, and knife blade towards the center of the plate angled at a 4:20 position.

Any unused silverware not picked up by the wait-staff is simply left on the table.

"There's no sincerer love
than the love of food"
George Bernard Shaw

Owning Real-Estate and Passing Food

Possibly you have always thought that real-estate is only related to land or buildings. While learning the rules of dining, I found out differently, and now it's your turn.

Your real-estate at a dining table consists of your dinnerware, silverware and glassware, and any dishes that are sitting directly in front of you. Your responsibility after sitting down is to take note of the various items sitting directly in front of you on the table. There may be:

- A Bread Basket
- The Butter Dish
- Salt and Pepper
- Salad Dressing, and Condiments
- Dishes of Food

You are responsible for any items placed in front of you. It is up to you to offer them to others at the table before or when asked.

Passing:
At the table, people will often ask: "Which way do we pass"? If this happens, say," to the right" and all should go well. With people laughing and sharing during dinner very few care otherwise. So, if you can get everything headed in the same direction, you'll do fine. However, there are "passing guidelines" and here they are.

To pass any item, pick it up with both hands and turn the handle away from you. Next offer it to the person on your left first, then pass to the person on your right. If you would like what you are passing, ask the next person if they mind if you first take a helping for yourself. If there are only two people at your table, offer whatever the other person wants across the table. If others at the table have immediately started passing to the left; smile and just go with it, knowing you know the rule for another time.

- Salt and pepper are always passed together.
- Turn handles toward the person you are passing to.
- Soupy items such as salad dressings and gravy are passed with the plate underneath.
- Butter, jams, etc. are passed in their own containers.
- If too many dishes accumulate in front of you, ask others at the table if you can move some near them.
- If someone is talking or eating and did not pass an item you want, ask again.

At a formal dinner food is served on a plate in appropriate portions. Second helpings are not an option. When dinner is served family or buffet style, it is perfectly fine to take a second helping.

How to Eat a Dinner Roll

In a recent "How to Eat a Dinner Roll" class I asked; "Does anyone know how to eat a dinner roll?" With a twinkle in his eye and a cheesy smile, one man in his 20's raised his hand. I daringly I called on him. "Matt" had everyone in tears laughing at his response.

He said, "Pick the bugger up, and put it flat in the palm of your hand.
Then grab a pat of butter with the other hand and open it.
Next using both palms, press the bread and butter together as hard as you can.
Smash 'em together if you need to.
Use both hands to stuff the roll in your mouth all at once.
Chew, n Chew, and Chew…
Lick your fingers and hands.
If you want another, look around and ask your neighbor if they want theirs".

Of course he was joking and everyone had a good laugh. Other classmates had different ideas of how to eat a dinner roll, while others sat wondering.

The best way to "Eat a Dinner Roll" is:
- When a bread plate is on the table, be sure to use it correctly.
- Touching only the roll you want, use your fingers to take it from the basket and place it on your bread plate located to the left of the dinner plate.
- If available, use a butter knife or the butter fork to take a curl of butter and place it on the bread plate.

At the Table

- Using your fingers is appropriate to take wrapped paper or foil butter pats to put on your plate.
- A dinner roll, bread, biscuit or muffin is not a hamburger bun, so should be eaten in small bites.
- Break off 2 to 3, one to two bite size pieces at a time.
- While holding it on the bread plate rather than above it, butter each bite sized piece when ready to eat it.
- Smaller biscuits do not have to be broken. It's never appropriate to cut a dinner roll with a knife.
- When rolls are served in a basket, take one then pass the basket to the right.
- Use your butter knife on your plate for spreading, not the butter server in the butter dish.
- The butter knife remains on the bread plate at the end of the meal.
- Eating rolls, biscuits and breads with jams and jellies is done the same as with butter.
- Once a piece the roll has touched your mouth, it should never go back on the plate.
- Hot rolls can be buttered at once before breaking off the two bite pieces.
- When buttering Toast or Bagels, there is no need to cut them into small pieces.
- Olive Oil is often served instead of butter. An extra plate will be brought to pour the oil on. If the roll is large, break off 2 bite size pieces to dip.
- When sharing olive oil on a plate, remember to never double dip your bread into the oil.

"Spaghetti can be eaten most successfully if you inhale it like a vacuum cleaner"
Sophia Loren

Table Talk

Have you ever had a conversation during a meal that was so pleasurable you didn't want to leave? Dinner conversations can be fun making the meal enjoyable or so heavy in conversation that you walk away hunched over with your knuckles dragging on the ground.

Recently while out of town on business, a friend asked me to meet for lunch or coffee. My schedule was tight and really didn't allow me to do so. However, since "Jon" once played an important role in my life, I made time to meet him, and was very glad I did.

Over the years regardless if it was one on one or in a group, when connecting with Jon it was as if he could only focus his thoughts and conversations on not liking his job, the concerns with his kids or a health concern. After enough conversations leaving me feeling as if my knuckles were dragging, I was at the point of not wanting to meet for coffee, let alone have food with him. This time was different. Immediately after sitting down in a quaint coffee house, Jon began sharing interesting stories. He talked of the recent changes he had made to his home, and a vacation he enjoyed the year before. He included me in the conversation by asking questions. We laughed, shared and spent quality time together. Lunch was pleasant and we both left feeling very good. Isn't that how everyone wants to feel?

This may sound harsh, however, in every interaction we have with someone we are trading valuable time that we could be doing other things. Everyone goes through rough times, and close friends can be there to help ride out the times. I was glad to see Jon, and know his life had finally turned around.

Encounters are brief and everlasting. When sharing time at the dinner table, people are making decisions if they want to spend additional time with you. They are also deciding if they want to refer you to someone for a job, a date, or for even a haircut. If you want to keep friends, and generate more while leaving a lasting positive impression, here are the tips to help you.

- Relax and keep dinner conversation light and enjoyable.
- Unless you are with your very best friend in a private setting, avoid topics such as religion, personal finances or your health.
- Invite others to talk by asking open-ended questions about their thoughts of a recently released movie, the latest book they read or what hobbies they enjoy.
- Ask opinions of a local new business or restaurant.
- In a group if the conversation becomes still, mention (big word…mention not elaborate) something humorous you recently read, or tell of a club or organization you enjoy and why. Next ask others if they have done the same.
- Listen with intent, adding only tidbits so others can elaborate.
- Remember the conversation killers of poor health, finances or broken heart stories.
- Realize you don't have to entertain, only initiate a conversation.

- Never take calls, text or check emails at the dinner table.

There are many interesting things to talk about instead of the mainstream topics of weather, or the food you are eating. Life can feel difficult at times, however shake things up and step away from it during a meal and enjoy! When listening with intent during mealtime, you will have fun plus learn many interesting viewpoints.

"I was eating in a Chinese restaurant downtown. There was a dish called Mother and Child Reunion. It's chicken and eggs. And I said, I gotta use that one."
Paul Simon

The Bill Cometh

Many years ago 12 people from the resort I was vacationing at went to dinner together. Deciding ahead of time the bill would be split equally, everyone had a great time laughing and relaxing as they ate dinner. Everyone shared in great conversations including afterward while having after dinner drinks. At the end of the evening, one man asked the waiter for the bill then brought out a tiny calculator. Everyone sat in disbelief as he divided the bill according to what each couple had ordered. It was both embarrassing plus extremely time consuming. In the end, there were variables of $3. to $5. between checks. Several people were openly offended. Was it worth it? No.

Many of us have experienced 'discussions' over who will pay the bill. People like to entertain and like to surprise one another by picking up the tab. Others prefer to split the check. To avoid concerns in paying the bill as in the story above, here are ways to manage situations before they occur.

When it comes to paying the bill, the guidelines are pretty straight forward: Unless agreed ahead of time, or meeting for fun with a friend; She or He who invites pays. Currently not standard in the US, yet widely spread across Europe; Chivalry is not dead, and men pay for the women present. Many people feel it is somewhat sad to see a couple split the bill after a romantic dinner. If dating, consider paying the bill in turns, as it may help to keep the fire going after a meal.

It is easy to sense uneasiness when the topic of money is raised. If someone insists on paying the bill offer to pay the tip, and pick up the tab next time. Many higher end restaurants have menus without prices so women or guests may feel free to order whatever they prefer without considering the cost. You can accept the status quo, or you may request all menus with prices on them.

When dining together, women will generally split the bill rather than dividing the bill individually by what was ordered. Men will do the same, or pay for everyone at the table.

In a group: At a special occasion such as a wedding, shower, birthday, or funeral, the host or hostess of the event pays the bill. When going with a group of friends and alcohol is served, ask for separate bills. Agreeing to do this ahead of time will keep the billing fair for everyone involved.

> "We must have pie.
> Stress cannot exist in the presence of pie."
> David Mamet

Money on the Table

Compared to the USA, Europeans have a different approach to paying extra for service given in restaurants. Never given to a restaurant owner, tipping shows appreciation for services rendered.

To avoid confrontations when paying the bill, arrive early at the restaurant and tell the wait-staff or Maître' de you will be paying the bill at the end of the meal. They may take your credit card numbers when you arrive or at the end of the meal.

In the USA, tipping is obligatory with the average between 15% and 20% because the wait-staff depends on tips for paying their earnings. In many restaurants and event centers for groups of 10 or more, a service fee of 18% is often added to the bill to cover gratuities.

In European Countries, rounding the bill isn't obligatory but a sign of showing one's way of appreciation for a service. Not required, the added amount may end up an additional 5% to 10%.

Done with discretion, tips may be left in the check folder or on the plate that comes with the bill. You can do so by adding to the amount paid by charge card, or give it in cash.

If you prefer to tip personally in cash, fold the bills in thirds and place it in the palm of your right hand. When you shake hands with the waiter or Maître' de, say, "thank you" as you pass the cash to them.

"One morning as I went to the freezer door, I asked my wife, 'What should I take out for dinner?' Without a moment's hesitation she replied, 'Me.'"
Anonymous

3.

After Dinner Bits and Bites

How to Make a Great Toast

Across the internet, in bookstores and libraries you will find 1,000's of ways to prepare a toast for any event. Giving a great toast is more than standing up after a few drinks and saying "I want to make a toast'. Here are eight easy steps in preparing a great toast, without people rolling their eyes while thinking "Oh my Gosh... please make him stop now!"

- Write a few ideas down to help you focus and organize your thoughts. It's been said that everyone has two voices, a spoken one and a written one. Once your ideas are in place; practice, practice, and practice. Practice first in the mirror, then later while driving in the car or doing things in the house. Rehearsing is the key, as it will help with the jitters plus help you feel confident knowing what you will be saying is what you want to express.
- Consider the audience, and their ages. Are they all adults, children, peers, or new people who are guests for the first time?
- Inside jokes should never be used unless it is a tight knit group of 6 friends.
- Embarrassment isn't a toast. Kindness and friendship are. Keep the information light, sincere, true and short. Never ramble when giving a toast. Keep it at 2 to 3 minutes total.
- Mean what you say, so speak from the heart. It will never lead you wrong. Any toast that evokes some type of emotion regardless if it's a lump in the throat, a tear or laughter is always on.

- Everyone knows funny stories; however, very few people are funny while saying a toast. Instead, just keep it light hearted.
- Keep the toast personal. If you know the people well, you'll speak from the heart and will know many good stories to tell. Pick one that honors them and will be meaningful to hear. Be yourself while telling it so it will reflect your sincerity for the event and people attending.
- Always remember, the best toasts are told from the heart.

"Food is symbolic of love where words are inadequate"
Allan D. Wolfelt

Invitations and Thank You Notes

Putting together a casual or an elaborate affair takes time, effort, and money. Invitations come in the mail, by phone, in person, and electronically. Regardless if the dinner is a formal or an informal affair, your response to an invitation should be given immediately or within three days. If you cannot respond within three days, do as soon as possible. If the invitation is in writing, take a week maximum from the time you received the invitation to respond. Responding to the invite will show respect to who invited you. This will also help the host and hostess to plan accordingly for food and beverages.

Invitations: Take notice of who is actually invited. Is it Mr. & Mrs.? Ms. & Guest?
Are children invited? Never ask or bring additional people who were not originally invited, including children.

Regrets only: When written on an invitation 'regrets only' means; only those who will not be attending need to reply. Always mail or call with your regrets. Doing otherwise, is just plain rude.

Additionally: If you have replied saying you cannot attend and your plans change; it is not proper etiquette to call and ask if you can still come. The host or hostess may have filled your spot with others they also wanted to invite.
Depending on the hosts, rules can be bent for a small private party in a home. Only if you know the host or hostess well, should you call and ask if you can still come. Once is enough, so expecting to bend rules should never become a habit.

Saying Thank You

Each of us know it's the smallest thing can have the largest impact either positive or negative. It's been proven by a fly in the room when one is trying to eat. Consider the feeling you have experienced when someone took time to write a handwritten note to say thank you. Wasn't it a nice feeling?

Taking time to write a Thank you note will leave a positive impression anytime. When written the day after the event, it adds waves of influence. Rarely does anyone make time to show appreciation in this way, so taking time to write a note of thanks in your own handwriting, will certainly make a class impression on the people who invited you. Writing a note only takes is a few minutes, with your favorite pen and a note card of your choice. Be honest, and use some extra creativity while remembering these tips.

- Write a thank you note within 1 - 2 days after the occasion, lunch, or dinner
- Keep the note short and to the point
- Start with a Greeting: Dear _____.
- Keep it light, and add some 'zip' to it, by mentioning something that took place in conversation or how much you enjoyed a particular food
- Thank them again for inviting you
- Sign and Send it!

Setting you apart from the crowd, know it is a true mark of respect to become skilled at writing thank you notes in this age of email, voicemail, and text messaging. So, why not write one?

> "Manners make a fortune of the ambitious person"
> Emerson

How to Eat Certain Foods

People often have questions of how to eat particular foods. I could write an endless list to help. However, here are most popular foods asked about in my "How to Eat a Dinner Roll" classes.

Asparagus
Often served with the main course, Asparagus can be eaten in two ways. If served cold as an appetizer without sauce, or with other vegetables on a vegetable tray, asparagus is eaten with the fingers. If served warm or in a sauce, cut it into portions and eat with a knife and fork. Leave any tough end pieces on the plate.

Artichokes
Artichokes are eaten with the fingers. Pull a leaf off the outside of the Artichoke, then dip the bottom of it into the sauce and pull it through your teeth to remove the edible portion. Place the remaining part of the leaf on the side of your plate or if one is provided on a separate plate. Scrape away the thistle with a knife and place it on the side of the plate. The artichoke heart is cut into pieces and can be dipped into the sauce and eaten with a fork.

Bacon
Only very crisp bacon should be eaten with the fingers. Otherwise, always use a fork.

Breakfast Pastries
Cut Danishes and other sticky pastries in half or quarters and eat with your fingers or a fork. Muffins should be halved with a knife and eaten with the fingers. If a muffin is warm, both halves may be buttered at once.

Cherry Tomatoes
I love cherry tomatoes. However, I suggest never eating them at a formal dinner party. When used for garnish they may squirt or roll two people away when poked with a fork or bitten into. Buy them for eating as a snack or on a salad at home, or at work and enjoy them there.

French Fries
When served with hamburgers and sandwiches, it is acceptable to eat French Fries with your fingers. In an upscale restaurant or when served with an entrée, cut them into pieces and eat with a fork. Do not smother French Fries with ketchup. Instead, pour a small amount at the edge of the plate to dip the fries in as you eat.

Grapefruit Halves
Eaten with a spoon, a chef will often loosen the sections before the grapefruit leaves the kitchen. When dining out, and finished eating the fruit, do not squeeze and drink the remaining juice from the rind.

Lemon Wedges
To add juice to food or beverages, while cupping your hand over the wedge, hold and pierce the lemon wedge with a fork. Next squeeze the juice onto your food. This will keep the juice from spraying someone nearby.

Olives
At cocktail parties, olives with pits are eaten with your fingers. The pits are then placed in a napkin or on a plate. At a dinner table olives are generally served without pits. They are eaten by rolling them onto a spoon. At the table if served with pits, the pits come out

the same way they went into the mouth, by using a spoon.

Poultry
In a restaurant, all poultry is eaten with a fork and knife. At a private home, or a casual outside BBQ, chicken legs, wings and thighs can be eaten by holding with your fingers. Anything larger should be eaten with a knife and fork. If you are casually dining at a sports bar and someone orders 'wings', stay casual and enjoy by eating them with your fingers.

Pasta
Separate long strands with a fork. Hold the prongs of the fork against the plate and twirl to gather the strands onto it. Never swirl in a spoon. Small-size pasta is eaten with a fork.

Potatoes
Baked potatoes are eaten with a fork. Potato skins should be eaten with a knife and fork. Add butter to a potato by taking butter from the butter plate with a clean fork. Never mash potatoes on your plate. Eat potato chips with your fingers.

Shrimp and Seafood:

Clams and Oysters Clams and oysters are served both raw and cooked. Both are presented on the half shell on a bed of cracked ice. The shell is steadied with one hand. A small seafood fork is held in the other hand to twist and extract the meat from the shell.

Raw Oysters: Served on a bed of cracked ice, they are often seasoned with lemon pepper or hot sauce. After removing the oyster from the shell with a seafood fork, quietly suck the loosened flesh from the shell. Afterward, lay the shell to the side of the plate.

Cooked oysters when served in casseroles and other various dishes are eaten with a fork.

Steamed clams: If a clam shell is difficult to open, or is tightly closed after being cooked, leave it alone. The clam is not good. Otherwise, hold the clam with the clam spoon given, and open it. Use the seafood fork to extract the meat. Dip the clams into clam broth or the melted butter served in a separate bowl. All discarded shells are placed in another bowl used for this purpose. When all the clams are eaten, if desired, the broth can be spooned from the dipping bowl or in a relaxed setting, drunk from the bowl.

Fried Clams: Deep fried, clams are greasy to eat with fingers so should be eaten with a fork. If rubbery when cooked, they may need to be cut before dipping them in a sauce given before eating.

Shrimp
Chilled shrimp are served in a stemmed glass with the tails left on. If the tails are in tack, eat the shrimps with your fingers or with a cocktail fork. If the shrimps are large without tails, use a fork and eat in 2 - 3 bites. If desired, move large shrimp one at a time to the serving plate below the stemmed glass and cut them before eating.

When shrimp are served fried, in casseroles, stir fried or cold in salads, they are eaten with a fork. Cut large shrimp before eating.

Soup
You want the soup coming to you, not you going to the soup. Sit up straight, and position yourself two hand widths from the table. Without hovering over the soup, lean slightly over. Place the soup spoon in the soup and scoop the soup away from you to the 12:00 position. To prevent drips, dab the bottom of the spoon on the edge of the bowl and eat the soup from the side of the spoon. If you are eating a hearty soup with meat or vegetables, the soup is eaten from the end of the spoon.

When finished, place the spoon on the plate below the bowl for the wait staff to take.

"Good Manners:
The noise you do not make while eating soup!"
Bennett Cherf

Cocktail Parties

Called "Cocktail parties" in the US and "Informal stand up parties" in Europe, the finger foods served at these affairs are often light and plentiful. The reasons for setting these events varies from 'just because' to a celebration reception or a business function. Knowing a few tips will help you to ease through any party as if it is second nature.

Before hand: Know why you are going to the event. Is it to meet new people, or possibly to honor someone or possibly just to have fun? If it's to meet new people, set a couple of goals to achieve while there. If you are very hungry before arriving, have a piece of fruit or a few nuts to take the edge off hunger. The purpose of going to any cocktail party should not be free food or unlimited drinks. Once you arrive, the bar or hors d'oeuvres table should not be the first place to stop. Meeting the host or hostess and mingling throughout the group should be your first priority.

Conversations:
Always hold your drink in your left hand, so your right hand is warm, dry and free to shake hands with. Mingle about, while keeping conversations light. Enjoy yourself. Do not talk excessively loud, and always give others a chance to talk. Keep the conversation light without saying sexual innuendos or off color jokes. Avoid topics such as health (yours or others), gossip, religion or politics. Always make eye contact when talking. Never just walk away from anyone without closing the conversation first.

How to Eat a Dinner Roll

Eating and Drinking:
At cocktail parties, never expect a full meal. Along with your drink or plate, always carry a napkin in your left hand.

At the food table take only a few items on your plate, and never overload it. After getting your food, walk away from the food table rather than standing near it. People will rarely notice if you take seconds, however they will notice a heaped plate. If a wait staff is there, excellent. Without plates available, take hors d'oeuvres one at a time. Avoid anything drippy, messy or very crumbly. Otherwise, there is a strong possibility you will visit the dry cleaners the next day.

If you are unsure if any of the food is too hot to enjoy, test the temperature by touching it with your tongue before biting into it.

If forks or other utensils are offered, use them. Chances are excellent you will shake hands with new people, and those you haven't seen in a long time. Honestly, who wants to shake hands with anyone who has salt, oil or a dipping sauce on their hands? And never, ever lick your fingers.

Beverage Etiquette:
During the event, pace yourself and limit alcohol drinks to one or two drinks.

Chilled wines and champagnes such as white wine should be held by the glass stem to keep the wine from warming. Red wines, brandy or scotch are served at room temperature or warmer, so the extra heat from your hand when holding the bowl or glass will enhance the bouquet.

To drink beer, pour it into a glass before drinking it. Alcoholic and non alcohol drinks are served predominately in non-stemmed glasses.

"I came from a family where gravy was considered a beverage"
Erma Bombeck

Extra Bits and Bites

Host and Hostess Gifts:
When dining in a private home, a nice gesture is to take a gift to the host or hostess. The gift doesn't need to be in the fashion of food or wine, but can be in forms of other gifts. Excellent examples of these gifts are: A music CD, a candle, a pack of note cards, printed napkins with small plates, gourmet jams or jellies, a box of candies or something meaningful to the host or hostess. With a meal planned if you bring unexpected food or wine it can put the host or hostess on the spot to serve it. If you take food or wine, tell the host or hostess it is for them to enjoy later. Flowers are always nice, especially when brought in a vase. This avoids needing to be attended to immediately possibly adding stress. Sending flowers a day ahead is always a good idea.

Remember: Taking a small gift to the dinner is a wonderful gesture, however does not excuse you from sending a thank you note a day or so afterward. (visit page 59)

If you're famished before a function:
If you haven't had time to eat during the day and dinner waits, eat something small before the event to take the edge off your hunger. A few almonds or a piece of fruit will do wonders, plus keep you from looking like a piranha at the event.

Helping Hands:
I recently went to an open house at a close friends' home. The couple had a fun, and relaxing night planned for friends with good food, wine and cocktails. Because not many replied to the RSVP, they estimated the turn out to be 20 to 25 people. Close to 45 people showed up that evening. Luckily, there was plenty of food and beverages. However the food, glassware and silverware needed to be refilled and the kitchen counters where the food was served attended to. The couple was buried in the sea of the evening, so a few close friends of the couple stepped forward to help. Other friends followed suit.

The rule of thumb is: Guests do not help with the duties of the evening. They are there as a guest. However, in particular situations there is a time to jump in. Only close friends and family members of the host and hostess should offer to help. In a small setting, that is a great rule. However, it is polite to offer your help any time you see the look overwhelm on a host or hostess' face. Simple gestures are powerful, especially in a time of overwhelm.

Think about it, in a situation like this wouldn't you want the help?

Wait-staff: When attending a formal dinner in a local area it is possible you may know some of the wait staff. It is always appropriate to say "Hello" or "Good Evening" while they are serving. If interested in carrying on a personal conversation with one of the staff members, do so after dinner and away from the table. Otherwise, the conversation disrupts their work, which is why they are there.

Grace and Religious Beliefs:
As we know, not everyone shares the same spiritual beliefs. When the host or hostess says grace, at the end you can remain silent, or quietly join in saying "Amen", "And so it is" or what you personally believe.

Dropsy's and Ooops!
We are human, and mistakes happen. At a private home, if you drop something pick it up, unless it is a purse, or napkin. When at a restaurant, leave it, and ask the wait staff to replace the spoon, fork, dinner-roll, napkin, or anything else that may drop.

If you spill something on the table use a napkin to blot it, then ask for a fresh one. If you spill red wine, blot only and do not rub. If a thick sauce or a butter tab is spilled, scrape it with your fork or knife and place it on your bread plate.
The wait-staff will take it from there. As a guest at a private home blot whatever is spilled and offer, to help the host or hostess while extending your apologies.

If you spill something on someone other than yourself, stop whatever you are doing and apologize. Get a napkin to give to them, and always offer to pay for any dry cleaning expenses.

Elbows, Wrists and Arms:
Were you ever told, "No elbows on the table while eating"? That is true any time you are dining. You can, however, rest your forearm (between the wrist and

elbow) on the table edge in-between bites and courses. Never lean on your arm while eating. Once the dishes are cleared away, having your hands, wrists or an elbow on the table is perfectly fine. Always be mindful you are not in anyone else's space when doing so.

With lips sealed Chew and Chew:
George Washington wrote in "Rules of Civility and Decent Behavior In Company and Conversation": "Put not another bite into your mouth till the former be swallowed. Let not your morsels be too big for the jowls."

Nicely said George, as who wants to watch someone eat huge bites of food as they roll around in their mouth and not be able to chew them? Ugh…

Cut three to four bites of your food at a time then eat each bite slowly with your lips sealed. Dining is fun. Unless the sky is falling, it isn't necessary to gulp food.

- Always sit up straight and never crouch or hover like a watchdog over your plate while eating.
- You will avoid smacking your lips if you chew with your lips sealed.
- Do not talk with food in your mouth. If someone asks a question, wait until you have completely swallowed your food before answering.
- Know loud noises such as slurping, groaning & moaning are as impolite as burping.
- Always cover your mouth when you cough. Use a napkin. If your hands are full, cough into your arm.
- Your body will love you if you don't overeat, or eat when upset.

- In the USA, fellow diners will love it if you do not wipe your plate clean by sopping up sauces or gravies with bread or a dinner roll.
- Your plate should never appear as it's been licked clean, plus it's always fine to leave a bite or two on your plate.

Grooming, Teeth and Lips:
Personal grooming such as combing your hair, blowing your nose (different from an unexpected sneeze), refreshing make up, lip-color, or picking your teeth should be done away from the table in the restroom.

Stand, say, "excuse me" or "I'll be right back". Place your napkin on the seat of the chair, and go take care of "business". When you return, sit down and join in the conversation that is taking place.

"I cook with wine, sometimes I even add it to food"
Julia Child

After Dinner Bits and Bites

"It keeps me from looking at my phone every two seconds."

Electronic Devices:
If you are dining with anyone other than yourself, turn off all electronics and share in the discussion taking place at the table. If you are waiting for someone to join you, or are on call for an emergency; with your phone on vibrate wait for the call, take care of business. Next, ignore all calls until after the meal. You will show those you are dining with they are more important than any phone call. This is priceless in any relationship.
It's simple: turn it off, or turn them off.

If, for any reason, you cannot miss a call, inform your host before the meal and take the call in another room. Keeping your phone on vibrate will never to disturb those around you.

Conclusion

I would like to thank you for reading "How to Eat a Dinner Roll". In this book, you have taken through the steps of arriving at a restaurant and a private home.

You have read how to take a seat, how to order, and now understand BMW, and tableware. You now know what to do with the napkin to prevent your dinner from being removed from the table when you have to leave the table momentarily. By now, you have a better understanding of passing food and dinner conversations.

You have also read how to pay the bill, and to share as a gracious host or hostess or as the guest. You have read the importance of thank you notes, and how to interact a cocktail party. In Extra Bits and Bites you learned extra tips of dining etiquette.

I've enjoyed writing this book, and hope you have enjoyed reading it. I invite you to contact me to facilitate the "How to Eat a Dinner Roll" class privately, to your family, or publically at your business, association, or place of worship. You will find the contact information in the following pages.

 I thank you again, and wish you many fun dining experiences filled with laughter, great food, and wonderful people.

Debra Carr

About the Author

Knowing appearance will take one only so far, in 1995 Debra Carr transitioned from a men's barber and salon owner to a certified image consultant. She offers image consulting, image coaching plus training programs. As the founder of Image for MEN, and Image Enhancement, she is recognized as 'the image expert for men'.

Debra is the recipient of Michigan's Barber of the Year award, also the former style and image expert for Northern Michigan's Men's Magazine. She has been awarded for excellence by BeautiControl Cosmetics, also recognized in print media. Along with Zig Ziglar, Malcolm Gladwell, and Robert Kiyosaki, Debra was interviewed by Portland, Oregon's "Tools for Success" talk radio, WLNS radio, and Grand Rapids, MI WTKG's "The Monica Sparks Show".
Her lists of clients vary from individuals of diverse backgrounds to Fortune 500 companies as Information Resource Group and General Motors, plus The State of Michigan, and the Prosecuting Attorneys Coordinating Council.

Debra believes in giving back to the community. She has given time to The Homes for Autism, Breast Cancer Walk of America, Mid-MI Cancer Wig Bank, Michigan's Bobby Crim Road Race, also the Athlete's of America inner city youth program. Currently she mentors a young girl, plus donates time at her place of worship.

As a known 'foodie' Debra spends her free hours with family & friends, at her love of gardening, capturing moments in photography, plus adding to her whimsical nose collection.

Quick Order Form

Mail, Fax or Call Orders
Debra Carr
Henry Carr Publishing
1120 Keystone Avenue
Lansing, MI 48911
office (810) 250-7331   fax: (517) 882-3433
email: debra@imageformen.net

Please send _____ copies of "How to Eat a Dinner Roll" We're sure you'll love it, if not, know if for any reason, it's returnable for a full refund within 30 days of purchase. No questions asked. To order: Please print clearly:

Name _____

Address _____

City _____ State _____ Zip _____

Phone _____

Email _____

Total books x $11.95 = _____ + _____ Shipping
Total Due: _____

Shipping USPS
Regular mail $4.00
Priority 2-3 days $7.00

Payment
Send check or money order: All orders shipped immediately..
Credit cards: please visit website or call our office to process

*For information on special discounts for bulk purposes, please contact the author via the above information.

**Signed copies available from the Author. Just ask, and include the recipients' name.

Consults, Classes and Coaching

The fun, informative and interactive class: "How to Eat a Dinner Roll" is available in various format sizes for individuals & family consults, to trainings for small to large groups at your business, association or place of worship.

To enhance your image further, Debra Carr is available for Image Coaching and Consulting services plus other Training sessions. To find out more you can contact her at:

Debra Carr
Henry Carr Publishing
1120 Keystone Avenue
Lansing, MI 48911

Office   (810) 250-7331
Fax: (517) 882-3433

Email: debra@imageformen.net
Image for MEN   www.imageformen.net
Image Enhancement   www.image-enhancement.us